PROPERTY SUCCESS

TOP 10 TIPS
TO SUCCESSFULLY

SELL

YOUR PROPERTY
@
AUCTION

PROPERTY SUCCESS SERIES

AUCTION SUCCESS:
TOP 10 TIPS
to SUCCESSFULLY
SELL
AT AUCTION

Property Success is a new book series teaching Australians how to successfully sell and purchase property at auction with confidence. Whether you are an investor, downsizer or buying your dream home, Maria Lawrance will guide you through the process to make selling a property by Auction a most positive and successful experience for both buyer and sellers.

Cataloguing-in-Publication entry

Lawrance, Maria, author.

Auction Success: Top 10 Tips to Successfully SELL Property at Auction
Series; Lawrance, Maria, Property Success ; 2.
Real property auctions—Australia.
House selling—Australia.

Dewey Number: 332.63240994

ISBN-10:   0992416523
ISBN-13: 978-0-9924165-2-2

Table of Contents:

Introduction

First Edition 2014 | Copyright 2014 by Maria Lawrance

INTRODUCTION

So you've heard all the hype about the incredible results some Auctions are getting but you're either:

terrified of the process and think you'll be forced to sell at a figure you're not happy with;

you're simply *scared* because you don't know what you're doing; you've had a *really bad experience* in the past that's put you off for life or someone you know has told you *horror stories* about their experiences that have seared into your brain ...

Well I'm going to dispel those fears and show you what an incredible system this can be, worked correctly, and if you are thinking of selling, you simply **MUST** give this system some serious consideration.

I am a Licensed Real Estate Agent and Auctioneer that has been selling Real Estate in the general area of Sydney, Australia for the past 27 years. I started auctioning properties just over 22 years ago and I have produced some amazing results for very happy clients, **regardless of market and economic conditions.** I believe an auction will always bring a better price for a property, but in a hot market, the result can be unbelievable!

Just this past year – 2013 – I have personally listed and auctioned 22 properties. Of that number, one property was withdrawn from sale (the owner changed his mind about selling) of the other 21 properties I achieved $1,188,000 over the reserve price for my clients! *An average of $56,571 per owner!*

That's like a good lotto win! Do you think my owners were happy with the results they got? You bet they were!

Just so you know, these were not my only listings and sales for that year. All up for 2013 I listed and sold 50 properties, so the majority were listed under the Private Treaty system. Of the 28 properties listed this way only **ONE** sold for more than the asking price, and that was only by $3,500 and only **ONE OTHER** sold at full asking price! All the other sales were **NEGOTIATED DOWN** which is standard practice with Private Treaty selling.

The Auction principles are Universal, only the bye-laws change from State to State in Australia and Internationally. It is these principles I am going to concentrate on and to teach you to understand them. I want to hopefully inspire you to rethink your fears, get expert advice and give this system a go!

Remember:

"For every feared thing there is an opposing hope that encourages us"

Umberto Eco

Chapter 1:
WHY AUCTION?

There are basically three methods that can be used to sell property. They are Private Treaty, For Sale by Tender or For Sale by Public Auction.

Private Treaty Sale

The most common method is for sale by Private Treaty. This is when the owner, or vendor, puts an "asking price" on a property which is usually set at a figure above what the owner would like to achieve, usually with direction from a Real Estate Agent taking into account recent local comparable sale prices, therefore allowing room for negotiation. The property is then marketed at this price and buyers that want the property will then make offers in accordance to the benchmark price that has been set.

Very rarely will an owner be offered more than that asking price or even at the asking price. The "game" is usually for the buyer to push that price down as hard as he can.

With this method of selling it is usual that the best offers are the first offers. The property is fresh to the market and will attract enquiry from buyers that may have been looking for some time and are ready to buy immediately. It is highly unlikely that any buyer will offer the full asking price, there is usually some negotiating down from that advertised figure. So it can be very difficult for an owner to accept an offer, even if that offer is at a figure that the owner first thought he would be willing to take. There will always be that nagging doubt "Did I sell too quickly?" "Did I let it go too cheaply?" "Is there a better price out there?" "What am I rushing for?" So many times I see this reaction from owners, and so many times I see these owners then selling for less than that original first offer! It can be an expensive education.

Regardless of market conditions every buyer believes that they are the only buyer on the property and they seem to make it their mission to get as much as possible off that asking price. They also want their terms and conditions met, such as, for example, a delayed settlement or a reduced settlement time. They may also insist that certain inclusions are added that were not in the contract, and their legal advisors will usually want a variety of changes to the terms specified in the owners' contract. These negotiations are usually done between the two parties (the buyers and the sellers) through a Real Estate Agent, who will be going backwards and forwards until a figure and terms are agreed upon. More often than not, the owners will have to capitulate on either their price or some of their terms if they want the sale to proceed.

Here in NSW most agents will not take a property "off the market" until a purchaser has signed a contract at the agreed price, or at their best offer. There are no "holding deposits" taken. The initial deposit has to amount to at least .25% of the purchase price, or the price offered. The agent will then take this signed contract to the owner and if the owner signs the counterpart contract, both contracts are dated and sent off to respective solicitors. This exchange is done with a cooling-off period which cannot legally be under five business days, but the cooling off time can be negotiated out further.

From the point of the contracts exchanging until the end of the cooling off period the owner is locked into that contract. He cannot change his mind about selling. He has to wait it out until the end of the cooling off period to see if his buyer can perform or even still wants to perform. This puts the owner in a very vulnerable position, particularly if he wants to purchase a property himself and needs the funds from this sale to complete his own purchase. If the purchaser changes his mind for any reason whatsoever, he does have to forfeit his original deposit (the .25%) to the owner, but often these monies are less than what the owner has to forego himself if he is upgrading to a higher price range.

Through the Private Treaty method there is no definite sale until the balance of the deposit monies are paid by 5 pm on the last business day of the cool off. This leaves the owner in limbo until this takes place and can cause a lot of stress to most vendors, particularly if they have committed themselves to another purchase. Should the sale fall through then the owner has to put the property back on the market and go through the whole agonising process again. In some unlucky instances, this may happen several times before a sale is actually finalised. By this time most owners' nerves are totally frazzled. And if this does happen what can also occur is that other savvy buyers will see the property back on the market and get even harder with their negotiations. The owner may then have no choice but to take a lesser figure than the previous sale price just to get the job done.

It has also been my experience that immediately prior to the balance of the deposit needing to be placed, some buyers will attempt to renegotiate the price once more. They may have found something in the building report that they can use as an excuse or really they will use any excuse to push the price down. I recently found out that a purchaser pushed a vendor's price down because a water tank that was never on the property when the buyer inspected the house had been removed. They firstly insisted on a $10,000 reduction – a truly ridiculous amount – which terrified the owner (who was committed to another purchase) so much that they eagerly agreed to a $2,000 reduction. Unfortunately I didn't find out all this had happened between the solicitors until after the event otherwise I wouldn't have let this happen.

No matter how difficult this form of selling is it is still far better than before this legislation came into effect. In some instances owners literally had to wait months before a sale became unconditionally exchanged (i.e. the 10% deposit went down and the buyers were locked into the purchase or would be made to forfeit that deposit). Back when I first started in Real Estate in 1986 and through most of the 90's a fully refundable deposit would be placed on a property and in some instances properties could be off the market for many months before the sale was formalised. Imagine the stress of that!

What also seems to be popular today in some areas is a Private Treaty sale but instead of a loaded price to work down, properties are being advertised with "Offers over ...." Personally, I really don't like this method, I think it is highly misleading, particularly when the owner's desired price is tens of thousands of dollars higher than the figure on display. For example a good client of mine wanted to achieve $600,000 on her property. A local agent advised her that to get this she needed to advertise at "Offers over $575,000" to draw a crowd and to let them pitch against each other. As a consumer myself if I saw that price heading I would expect that an offer of $576,000 should stand a chance, not that I would have to pay at least a further $25,000 to get the property. I advertised this property at $629,000 and sold it in one day for $620,000. I doubt that the "offers over $575,000" formula would have led to a further $45,000 being offered!

For Sale by Tender

The For Sale by Tender method is very similar to the Auction system except that buyers' bids are not disclosed to each other. A date will be set for all offers to be submitted and then the vendor will accept what he considers to be his best offer and terms. The successful bidder is then notified. No-one has the opportunity to make more than one bid otherwise the agent can be accused of instigating gazumping, which is illegal and can cost an agent thousands of dollars in fines and they can also lose their Licence.

What has recently become very popular, particularly in the Western Suburbs of Sydney, is a For Sale by Tender, but called a Property Launch or a Home Drive. What happens in this instance is that a property is advertised with a price range and a set open house time. No buyers will be allowed to inspect the property prior to this time frame because, again, the agent wants each buyer to see a lot of activity at the property. This will hopefully convince the buyer that there is strong competition for the property which can result in offers at the higher end of the price range or even over the price range if they are very keen.

Usually there is no more than a $30,000 play in the price range advertised such as $430,000 to $460,000, with the desired sale price approximately half way between these two figures. I have tried this method of selling and I can say it does work. However, having parameters on the price range again limits the thinking of the buyers, and in a rapidly rising marketplace, which is what we are enjoying in Sydney right now, this may prevent buyers from really stretching to get the property. And often there will be exactly the same figure offered several times, which makes me believe that if each buyer were aware of that, surely one of them would have paid more to get the property? Under these circumstances the owner then has to make a decision between buyers, particularly if the terms of sale are also identical.

Usually when offers are submitted through this system they are done so still with a cooling off contract and the sale is still not unconditional at the point of the owner accepting the offer. Once again the owner is in a vulnerable position.

For Sale by Public Auction

From my extensive experience I can wholeheartedly say that this sale process is the most efficient, fairest and by far the most transparent mode of selling that I have encountered.

First of all, the standard time frame for an Auction campaign is usually four weeks. During that time as many people as possible are shown the property. This can be through the weekly open houses or by appointment through the weeks leading up to Auction day. Setting the date deadlines the sale and gives both buyer and seller time to prepare for the event. This takes away any anxiety that the property has sold too cheaply or too quickly. Owners can see the volume of inspections being done and can feel safe that the very best price is going to be available on the day of the Auction.

Most importantly, when the hammer comes down at the Auction the property is SOLD! There is no cooling off contract, it is a definite sale at a definite price. Obviously this is very powerful for the owner. Buyers are at liberty to bid to whatever price they deem the property to be worth, but the competition is no longer against the owner and to drive his price down. The competition is to beat the other bidders and secure the property.

The terms and conditions of purchasing the property are in the Contract for Sale that the owners' solicitor has prepared and they have to be adhered to by the buyer. The buyer has the opportunity to take this contract to his own legal advisors prior to the Auction and occasionally the buyers' legal advisor will contact the sellers' solicitor to have some terms amended – but never as much as a Private Treaty sale, I've noticed.

All in all, this system puts the owner back in the driving seat, rather than the other way round. What I particularly like is that most lending bodies will take an Auction sale price as a current valuation. We are in an upwardly moving marketplace and often Property Valuers are instructed by lending bodies to look at recent **SETTLED** sales, not exchanged sales, for their benchmarks when valuing a property. These sales may have happened quite a while ago and can be considerably under immediate recent sales results. Consequently we are seeing buyers lose out on what they want if the Property Valuer comes in at a low assessment. I have recently had a purchaser agree to a purchase price of $740,000 for one of my properties. A valuer went through this property and came up with a valuation of $670,000! Fortunately the buyer did not accept this valuation and instructed his broker to change banks. The new valuer came in at $740,000, no problem, and the sale went through. I don't know how there can be a variance of $70,000 between valuers, and certainly the $670,000 figure didn't make any sense at all, but an Auction result would never have led to this outcome.

All of the above points show explicitly why this method is superior to a Private Treaty sale. I think that the reason Auctions have the edge over For Sale by Tender Sales is simply because each bidder can see what the opposition is doing, instead of trying to outguess the next person. This builds buyers confidence in the property and can encourage a stronger result for the owner.

Also, there are no restrictions with an Auction sale. Let's face it, there is no scientific formula for pricing a house. Each property is totally unique and even though there may be strong comparables between houses, there can also be undetermined reasons one house is more popular than another. And that popularity can only mean one thing … a better price for you!

Tips from this chapter:

1. There are three basic methods of selling – but Auction is by far the best!

2. You have control of the sale. It's your terms and your conditions.

3. Buyers at Auction are pitching against each other not YOU!

4. Banks/lending bodies are more likely to accept an Auction result as a valuation.

5. When the hammer comes down you are SOLD! No further negotiations!

Chapter 2:
Your Motivation

Why do you want to sell your property? Are you looking to upgrade, downgrade, cash in an asset, get out of debt, end a partnership, relocate or retire to a different area? Has the recent media storm regarding the rise in home values stirred up moving needs in you? Have you done this before, or are you fresh meat to the shenanigans of selling your home? Personally I have sold and bought 12 different homes to live in in my lifetime, which is the exception not the norm. However I believe that my own personal experiences of the whole traumatic process has made me a far better real estate agent. I KNOW what it's like to be on the receiving end of what I do as a job!

Your motivation for why you are selling is absolutely crucial, so work out from the headings below which category you fall into.

"I'm not that motivated, but if I get my price I'll sell"

If you're not that motivated, then you probably don't think Auction is right for you. You just want to put the property on the market with a price that will test the waters. Normally half-hearted sellers will want well over market value and will only sell if they get an unusually high price. However, you may be pleasantly surprised in a rapidly rising market: you may just get your Dream Price! So even if this is you, have plan B ready to go if this occurs.

I believe that even if you are not that motivated you should be willing to go through the Auction process, invest some of your own money in the promotion of your property, to test those waters. It's your choice entirely, but certainly if you really want to get your dream price and won't sell for less, then an Auction will draw out the maximum worth of your property. You don't have to sell if you're not happy with the result, but it will shorten your time on the market to find out what the market thinks of your property's value.

Do you really want to spend the next several months having people traipse through your property to then tell you "it's too dear!" or do you want to condense this into a month and find out the result quickly?

"I want to upgrade/relocate area but I haven't found what I want to buy yet"

If this is you then you're probably scared that you may get a buyer on your home and have nowhere to go to. Understandable. But, what if you keep seeing homes that suit you but you're not in a position to buy and no-one will wait for you? How committed are you to making this move?

If you are absolutely sure you are moving but you cannot commit to anything until you have sold yourself then put your property up for Auction with a longer settlement period! Instead of the standard 6 weeks from exchanged contract to settlement, make it 12 weeks, or longer. This will then give you time to sell your property and then it will give you time to look, find and secure the home you want. And whilst your own Auction programme is running, go out and look at properties yourself. You will be getting regular feedback on what buyers' are thinking your home is worth and you will have better knowledge of what you can afford to spend.

Should you be relocating to a completely fresh area such as Interstate, the Coast etc. then I would strongly advise to rent before you buy anyway. The last thing you want to do is rush to buy in an area you are completely unfamiliar with and end up with a nice home surrounded by Housing Commission properties! You would be far better off to rent for six months and get a feel for the area before you commit to a purchase. You also need to get a general idea of prices in this new area. When moving away from a large city, such as Sydney, to a country/coastal/new State you will generally find prices of properties are much lower, and what may appear to be a bargain compared to your home values could actually be an over inflated price locally. Don't get burned.

Does this still feel too risky to you? No problem. Go to your bank and discuss **Relocation Loans** with them. If you have a substantial amount of equity in your own home, generally have a good income, the chances are that you will be able to borrow the full purchase price plus all costs (such as Stamp Duty and solicitors fees). This will allow you to go out and buy before you sell and take away the feeling of vulnerability for you. Usually there is a time frame with this type of loan which will allow you to then sell your property, and the interest rates for this loan are usually at the same variable rate as a standard Home Loan. Once your property sells then the equity in your existing home will come off the whole amount which will either clear your debt completely or reduce it to a much lower figure. Then you need to Auction your own home to safely secure a sale within the right time frame. There is usually a set-up fee for this loan, but all this you need to discuss with your bank/lending body.

"I've already bought/built and I need to sell!"

If you are a fully committed vendor with high motivation then Auction is the only method to consider. Why? Well first of all if you are committed to another purchase and you need the funds from this house to pay for the next one you need a definite time frame to work in. The Auction campaign will do that – four weeks for the programme and then your own specified time for settlement. Remember, you are in control of those terms in your contract, so instead of a standard 6 weeks to settlement from exchange, you can reduce this to 5 or even 4 weeks thus reducing your waiting time for those funds to come to you. And when you set the Auction date you are really setting your sold date!

If you have to sell quickly then Auction will allow you to do that without necessarily compromising your price. A quick sale can often result in taking less just to make things happen. An Auction will draw out your best price regardless.

I look at price ranges for properties as being three-tiered: "Ouch!" price, if this is all you can get this hurts your plans, "Reality" price, probably what your property is really worth, "Dream" price, if you get this for your home you are ecstatic! A quick sale, or fire sale, will usually result in either an Ouch or Reality sale price. You are under the pump to sell and you are not in a position to negotiate hard. You care too much!

What can be even worse is if you do go through the Private Treaty process, find a buyer and then that sale falls through, you are even more under the pump than ever before and your property's price may be compromised further. Or you could be so trapped into the sale that should the buyer put pressure on you immediately prior to the end of the cool-off you may be forced to drop your price again or stand to lose the buyer. Not a strong position to be in.

Just remember the Golden Rule of Auction: **"Caveat Emptor!"**

Buyer Beware! Simply put it is up to the purchaser to make their own enquiries and have inspections (pest and building reports etc.) done on the property prior to purchasing at Auction. If this is not done, or even if this is done and the buyer isn't happy with these reports but still goes ahead and purchases, he cannot then demand that the owner be responsible for any repairs that may need to be done to the property. The hammer comes down, that price is paid and the property is SOLD! No ifs, buts or maybes after the event. Done deal, thank you very much.

"We're divorcing/selling a Deceased Estate"

Whether it's the death of a loved one or the death of a marriage, this means that there are generally several parties involved and there can be conflict between them.

With a divorce obviously there could be acrimony between two parties which can affect sensible commercial decisions.

Auctioning a property can overcome these difficulties provided that a smart reserve price is put on the property.

In the case of a Deceased Estate not only can there be conflict between beneficiaries that may increase when offers are submitted, but there is also a need to honour the memory of the person that has passed away. With an Auction you will know that you have done your very best to obtain the most out of the market – parents or family members have worked hard to leave you this legacy – they would want this.

"I'm cashing in an investment while the prices are good"

OK. First question: have you checked with your Accountant/Financial Advisor regarding the amount of Capital Gains Tax you'll be up for? Here in Australia if you purchased a property post 1985 and that property is sold at a greater price than what you paid for it, you will have to pay this tax. I am not going to go into that arena here, I am not trained to give financial advice, but I am going to point you to the right direction to find out if this applies to you and the consequences that may occur should you sell. It could be that you have to plan this a little better and wait for a certain time of the year. Get the correct advice and heed it.

Once you have researched your situation then I am also going to recommend auctioning the asset to you. If the property is vacant then you really don't want it off the market for too long – chances are each month will incur expenses such as mortgage repayments, rates, maintenance etc. Or it could be vulnerable to vandalism by being vacant. So deadline the sale and maximise your return.

Should the property be occupied by a tenant then an auction campaign should synchronise better with that occupant allowing inspections. Just a short time on a Saturday is far preferable than random inspections. And again, the best possible price will be obtained.

"I've got to sell – I can't afford to stay here!"

In this instance the quicker you sell the better. Every month you stay on the market you are keeping an asset you cannot afford. Each month is another mortgage repayment and you get further in debt. If you've stopped paying your mortgage you are drawing closer and closer to the bank stepping in and taking the property off you.

Should you be in this position then get your property on the market immediately. Most certainly an auction is the way to go. Let your lending body know what action steps you have taken. They will also prefer an auction because this deadlines the sale and they will have a definite time frame to work with. If you find a good agent they will contact that lending body and will keep them informed throughout the selling process. This will keep the wolf from the door. Don't stick your head in the sand – grasp the nettle!

A few years ago I was approached to sell a parcel of land that had a slab poured for a duplex. The owner of the land had entered into an agreement with her sister that she would supply the block of land and the sister and her family would build a duplex. They would then share the profits equally once the two properties were built and sold. A great plan, and should have worked perfectly.

Unfortunately the owner of the block of land had a compulsive gambling habit and the stage payments that had been made to her by the bank to fund the building project were sunk into poker machines at the local RSL rather than into the construction of the duplex. The concreter that had laid the slab hadn't been paid, the initial mortgage on the land hadn't been paid, the rates hadn't been paid and there were no further funds to finish building the dwellings. A fine mess.

I knew the circumstances were dire so I listed the property to Auction and then spent the following four weeks promoting and showing the property as is my job. I arranged for the two sisters to come into my office the day before the auction to set the reserve price. The owner of the block came in with handfuls of unopened mail from the bank she was with. She was in such a deep hole she didn't even have the wherewithal to open her mail, so I did it for her. It was at that point that we all discovered that the bank had already moved on her and repossessed the property!

Long story short, I got onto the bank and got a stay of execution. I took the property to auction the next day and got the absolute most out of the buyer. We did not exchange under auction conditions (we raised the reserve price to a figure that cleared all debt which was a considerable amount over market value). I obtained a signed contract off that buyer with the 10% deposit, explaining to him that he needed to wait for an answer and if it was a "yes" then the exchange would be under cooling off terms. I then got hold of her Superfund, applied for a release of some funds because of her extenuating circumstances, filled out forms and got the evidence of the debt she was in and managed to get sufficient funds released to clear all her remaining debts. If the bank had gone through with the repossession they would have auctioned the property as a fire sale and most likely would have sold the property at a much lower figure than I achieved. There would have been further interest charges from the take-over to the sale end and all the costs associated with the sale would have been passed on to the owner. So even though the property would have been taken off the owner, once the property is sold the owner is still responsible for the shortfall between the sale price and all debts to the lending body. She would end up with an extremely bad credit rating and still have been in debt to the concreter, local Council et al.

So, don't stick your head in the sand. If holding onto your property is ruining the quality of your life and sinking you further into debt, grasp the nettle, get it sold, and get back onto solid ground. And do it quickly whilst you still have some leverage.

Avoid a repossession at all costs, the consequences stay with you for a very long time.

Tips from this chapter:

1. No matter what your motivation an Auction is a suitable way to sell

2. You retain the control of the sale throughout the Auction process

3. The terms and conditions of your Contract can be set to suit your needs

4. Do your homework – get legal advice or financial advice first and foremost

5. Do you want to deadline the sale of your home without sacrificing your price? Then take your property to Auction!

Chapter 3:
Choosing an Agent

You are about to put your most valuable asset on the market for sale. This is the epicentre of your wealth. You have probably toiled extremely hard to buy, maintain and pay off this property. And you are about to put it into someone else's hands to liquidate it as an asset. Choose them carefully!

I compare my trade to any other that's out there, but I like to use the analogy of woodworkers:

Tradesmen: these are fairly competent woodworkers with some knowledge and skill. They can get a job done, albeit roughly, and they are fairly cheap. This is a job and they are doing it to earn a living. The quicker they get paid the better, so they won't waste time on finesse, but rather they like to be in and out quickly. Near enough is good enough, what do you expect for this kind of money?

Carpenters: they are more skilled than a tradesman, they are working with wood every day. They are usually a little more expensive than a tradesman. The job they do is above average, moderately expensive, but adequate. They will also focus on quantity rather than quality, but they do take more pride in the end product.

Cabinet makers: they know every tool in their kit and know when to use them appropriately. They know their wood. They know every knot, every twist, and every possibility of what that wood can achieve. They love their work and every piece they turn out is done with a level of care and concern that has taken years of dedicated training to achieve. They are expensive, but the quality of their work is unsurpassed.

When you start interviewing agents try fitting them into the above categories. The lesser skilled agents will not discuss various methods of selling your home, they just want the listing. Often they will not talk about your needs, but they will focus on impressing you with their achievements or their office's achievements. Some agents won't look at the different angles that they can use to promote your property to get the very best price – they will want to know what you want for the property. When I am at an initial interview my focus is very much on "what are the needs of these owners?" so I ask a lot of questions to find out their motivation, their dreams and I then dovetail what I can offer to synchronise with their plans. For me, the needs of my clients are far more important than anything else. If I fulfil these needs to the very best of my ability, the money will always follow.

Most legal advisors will tell their clients to get three agents out to look at their property. I suggest you get as many as you wish until you find the agent that you feel most comfortable with, that gives you their track records of what they have achieved and that can talk with knowledge and experience regarding your property, the local area and their recent sales results.

Track Records

So, what do you need to know? I believe that two of the most important statistics you need to see are a) how many properties has this particular agent sold in the past year and b) what were the average sale prices from what he told his clients he'd get them to what he actually got for those properties.

Personally I have sold 106 properties in the past 106 weeks, at the point of writing this book. My sale price to agent's opinion rests at 99.83% across all those properties. What does this mean? Well it means that I am very active in my marketplace and that I am extremely accurate on my assessment of value.

A genuine and accurate assessment is so important to anyone thinking of selling, particularly if you are going to base your next move on the funding you get from this sale. Unfortunately inexperienced owners do get seduced by agents offering huge prices for the property that are not grounded on any substance. We have a saying in the trade that often "the biggest liar at the lowest commission gets the job." Don't be fooled by this.

A good agent will bring a number of comparable sales with them when they come to assess your property. They will also show you similar results that they have obtained for properties in close proximity to yours. They will then explain the differences between your property and the sold properties, giving you both the pluses and the minuses between these properties. They should also be able to have an instinct for what they believe your property is worth, based on their experience and recent demand. So if an agent tells you something that you find too good to be true, it probably is.

When I assess a property I always look at comparable sales. I then check out how many similar properties are on the market to compete with this home. I then make a check list of all the benefits that this particular property has compared to the other stock, and what may be seen as its shortcomings. I then draw on my instincts and experience as to what I believe I can achieve for this property. And I'm not often wrong!

Personally I would rather under quote and over deliver rather than the other way round. But what I prefer to do is be true to my word: if I tell you I'm going to get you a certain figure then that's what I'll do. And if I can exceed this, you bet I'm going to go for it!

Attitude

Probably the most important trait you should look for is attitude. How enthusiastic is this agent to get your business? How does he respond to your property? Does he point out the benefits and appear to recognise its selling features? Is he/she keen to get your business? Sometimes raw enthusiasm can be slightly better than skill levels. Combine passion with skills and you have probably just found yourself a champion performer.

Personally, I really don't like arrogance, and I find this to be an unfortunate trait in any agent. A client's needs should always be far more important than anyone's ego. The years have taught me humility – "be gracious in your defeat and be humble in your victories" is a mantra that I have adopted. I am truly amazed the number of times I hear from clients that they have been "told off" by an agent for not choosing them!

The Commission

I deliberately left this subject to the last because I sincerely believe it should be the least of your considerations when choosing an agent. Their abilities, skills, experience and attitude are so much more important – or should be!

However many owners that I have met over the years are more obsessed with what an agent will charge rather than what an agent is prepared to do to get them their very best price. Your home is probably your most valuable asset. You have worked hard, saved hard, compromised on your luxuries to get this home and to look after this home. Why would you then look for cheap, cheap when the time has come to cash it in?

Imagine this: you have just been diagnosed with a serious heart condition. The Heart Specialist you've seen shows you that he is really good at dealing with this condition but he is going to charge you $20,000. Would you then go to a vet because he'll only charge you $8,000???? Of course not! Then don't choose an agent based on how low you can screw down his fees!

Just remember, the cheapest agent isn't the one with the lowest commission – he's the one who will get you your very best price! And not all agents will do this. The difference between a good agent and a mediocre agent may be ½ or 1% in commission, but this could mean tens of thousands of dollars for you! The average sale price around Sydney right now is approximately $660,000. 1% of this is $6,600. If the average money I got for my auction vendors last year came in at $56,571 **over their reserve price**, don't you think that investment of an extra 1% was worth it to them? They still ended up being $50,000 better off!

Furthermore, how skilful is an agent if he can't even negotiate a reasonable fee for himself? If he is such a weak negotiator that he can't get himself a decent commission, what do you think he is going to do with the sale of your home? How do you think he is going to handle the hard-ass buyers that he's going to be bringing through your property? A weak agent with a low commission isn't going to care about **how much** he's going to get for you. He's more concerned with **how quickly** he can get paid!

This is what happened to me. Back in 1979 I was living in England. My then husband was a builder and we had earned very good money for several years. We had two gorgeous young children and a comfortable double storey home on a one acre block in the beautiful foothills of Malvern, Worcestershire in England. Life was sweet. But we always yearned to live on acreage. That was our dream.

So we went and bought a large cottage on 16 acres of land close to a village called Bromyard in the heart of Herefordshire countryside. We arranged bridging finance through our bank and bought this property at auction. At that time bridging finance was very similar to a relocation loan, the major difference however is that bridging finance was 5% over the variable interest rate at that time, so it was a dangerous position to be in, but we felt very confident that we would sell quickly and not have to carry this debt for too long.

My then husband was a hard-ass when it came to negotiating. After interviewing several agents we put our property on the market with the local agent who had allowed my husband to heroically screw down the commission to 1%.

As a result we hardly ever saw this guy. He would send the buyers directly to us and I would show them through the house. He rarely gave us feedback, and the only time we really heard from him was when our advertising monies had been used up and the account needed topping up.

Within two weeks of coming on the market we got our first offer on a Monday morning after a Saturday inspection. We had listed the property at £55,000 pounds. We ideally wanted £53,000 pounds. The offer came in at £51,000 pounds.

We gave serious consideration to this offer overnight and, believing that as this was their first offer they would be bound to pay more, we rejected it. We really thought we knew it all. We then sat and waited to hear their counter offer. And we waited. And we waited. And we waited. By the end of the week we could wait no more and we rang our agent.

"Oh, yes, you mean those cash buyers from Guernsey? No, they won't be making a counter offer. When you rejected their offer they went ahead with their second choice of property. That owner didn't hesitate in taking their offer" he informed us.

Can you still hear our stunned silence?

Soon after we rejected this offer the newly elected Margaret Thatcher government, in their wisdom, raised the interest rates to 17%, which meant that we were now paying 22% on our bridging finance, and this interest was compounding every month. Nationally we went into one of the worst recessions ever experienced in England. It took us nearly two years to sell this house, and when we did we sold it for ….. £51,000 pounds! But by then we had lost over half the equity we had in our home. Our marriage never really recovered from the terrible financial pressure we put on ourselves, and shortly afterwards we went through a very difficult divorce.

However the upside to this experience has made me a very, very savvy real estate agent. From this experience the lessons I learned have been invaluable to me in this career. First of all, when I put in an offer to any of my vendors I give them the full picture of the buyer. The buyer's circumstances are crucial for an owner to make an educated decision. I also keep my vendors fully informed of the buyer's thinking – if they are going to make a simple choice between two properties then the owners of both those properties need to know that.

I also learned that if you are going to pay peanuts, you are going to employ monkeys. For all I know our agent could have been half decent if he was going to be paid half decently. I believe he didn't try too hard to sell our property to the "Guernsey cash buyer" because the commission on the other property was probably a lot more attractive. He was looking after himself, not us, and that's as much our fault as his.

But more importantly, I learned that had we taken our own property to auction, none of this would have happened and we would have been sold before the bridging finance kicked in and before the interest rates rose to a ridiculous level. We didn't choose auction simply because we didn't want to pay the auction fees.

Testimonials

Ask for reports from these agent's other clients! Personally I obtain feedback from every single owner I sell for. I usually get another staff member to ring the owner after a property is unconditionally exchanged and to ask for their straightforward feedback. Of the past 106 sales, each owner has been very happy with the service, feedback and outcome. This is more important to me than anything else.

Finally ...

Do you really want to know how your agent is going to perform once he has your business? Then ring his office as a **buyer enquiry** and assess the response time! Discuss a property that he is promoting and see how he handles that enquiry. Does he give too much away? Is he enthusiastic about that property? Does he try and make an appointment with you to see the home? Does he ask you any qualifying questions over the phone? How enthusiastic is he to help you? Because that's what he's going to be like when he's working for you!

Tips from this chapter:

1. Interview several agents and categorise them according to their skill levels

2. What are the agent's track records like? Does he even keep them?

3. How enthusiastic is this person to get your business? How enthusiastic is he to get you the very best price, and what are his strategies?

4. How strong/weak is he when discussing his commission? Did he drop his rate quickly? Will he do this with your price?

5. What do his past clients think of him? Has he bothered to keep any testimonials or feedback from these clients?

6. Before you even get an agent out to interview him, approach him as a buyer enquiry either over the phone or at an open house and check out his responses.

Chapter 4:
Marketing your Property

Every agent you deal with will have prepared Marketing Programmes for their Auction Campaigns, provided that they are Auction friendly agents. If they are not Auction friendly, then I would be cautious of their skill levels.

Usually these campaigns are three tiered and called something like "Bronze", "Silver" "Gold" or similar. And the campaign fees will increase with each package, depending on the extras included. Marketing packages will vary between different suburbs and States depending on the use or not of print advertising.

The standard campaigns comprise of professional photography, Virtual Tours and floor plans; advertising on the major internet sites; sometimes print advertising in local papers; personalised signboards with photographic displays of internal features of the property; professionally produced leaflets of the property and, of course, the Auctioneer's fee.

With the advent of Internet advertising a lot of print advertising has been made obsolete in many suburbs close into City centres. It was always extremely expensive in these areas and now is certainly not essential for a good marketing campaign.

There are several major internet sites that serve us here in Australia such as realestate.com and domain.com. I like a presence in both as they are both high traffic portals to properties. Both sites, for extra fees, will allow a property to be featured as a header on the front page of the site for a particular suburb. Sometimes these fees will be part of the auction campaign packages being offered to you.

I truly believe that if you are going to take a property to Auction you need to broadcast this as wide and as far as you can. You want to capture every single person looking to buy in your price range, and you want them to come through your property. If you are prepared to spend some money on preparing your home for market – and I meet a lot of home owners ready to paint and recarpet their homes to make them look more attractive to buyers – then spend some money on widely promoting your property to get the heads through the door! Agents will have standard amounts they can invest in the promotions, but no agent is going to invest thousands of his dollars into your home's promotion – that is for you to do. It doesn't have to be thousands but it will be money well spent!

Whichever auction campaign you choose, they will all have a four week lifespan. Standard procedure is to hold an open house each Saturday at the same allotted time. With on-site auctions (auctions that are actually held at the property) the actual auction usually takes place immediately after the last open house. With in-rooms auctions (groups of properties are put together and auctioned in possibly a community hall, at a local club or in the agency's office) the auction is usually held on an evening (Thursday evening seems to be popular) after the last Saturday open house.

With in-room auctions an "order of sale" will be available on the night showing the order that the auctioneer is going to call the auctions. Standard practice, if there are several properties up for auction on the same night, is to have the most popular at the beginning and at the end so that good results are obtained at the beginning to set the mood for the evening and then also to keep the crowd in the room. When I used to call auctions for other agents I have called as many as 20 auctions in one night! As you can imagine, I didn't spend too much time on each individual property – there just wasn't the time to do this. We would start at 7 pm and we had to be finished by 11 pm – that's when the room closed. So that meant calling 5 auctions per hour. Doable, certainly, but very little individual attention to each property. In-rooms auctions will have videos of each individual property playing immediately prior to the auctioneer starting to call that particular auction.

Personally I prefer on-site auctions. The reason I do so is because I allow at least an hour for each property. I can spend time talking with owners so that we can plan our strategy (more about that later), then I can call the auction. I am not under pressure to move on to the next property, so I can really make sure I extract the juice for my owner before I bring the gavel down.

With in-rooms auctions, my attention is to get through the volume of properties. However, I have to say that occasionally with in-room auctions buyers may start bidding on properties they haven't physically seen! I have had several "sight unseen" sales at these venues. Usually a buyer that has missed out on an earlier auction will stay in the rooms, sees something else he quite likes and then starts to bid. He has come to the venue to buy and that's exactly what he does! It can be dangerous, because he hasn't done his research, may not know the location or if there are any detrimental aspects to the property, and is taking quite a risk. There is nothing detrimental to the owner; "Caveat Emptor!" Buyer Beware!" He has sold, and that's all he wants to do.

I can unequivocally say that selling "sight unseen" only ever happens with an Auction. With any other form of selling it is unheard of. It usually takes several inspections with a Private Treaty sale for the buyer to make an offer and even then they have a cooling-off period in which they can change their minds.

Going back to the marketing of your property please remember this: the initial impression a buyer is going to have of your property is through the promotional or marketing material. It needs to be sharp, well written, well photographed and prominently displayed. It needs to capture the main selling features of your property and it needs to create urgency or the willingness to act within the buyer.

The heading of the ad really needs to capture, in just a handful of words, enough interest to make a buyer find out more about the property and the reason it's for sale. Some agents will use an opening bid or starting bid on a flash on the photo. This can be most useful to draw a crowd. Usually the opening/starting bid is approximately 10%-20% under the anticipated sale price, but it can direct the right interest to the property and is a good benchmark to give buyers so that they can check if the property is within their budget.

The owner's reason for selling is also important as it will show the buyer how motivated you are. All buyers want to make sure that owners will be realistic in their expectations on the day of the auction, otherwise there is no point in attending the auction. They may be willing to pay a big price through the competitive bidding, but they want to know that they do stand a chance of buying the property, so they do like to be given guidelines. The best auction results are usually obtained when the owner's expectations are similar to the crowds. That's when the competitive bidding really does kick in.

Probably one of the best auctions that I remember was one in the late 1980's of a property that was in a flood affected area local to my office. The owner was moving to Townsville and wanted a quick sale. I assessed the property to be worth approximately $100,000 to $110,000 at that time. The owner told me he was very happy to take $95,000 as this sum would enable him to do what he wanted.

I've never been the sort of agent that would simply go and get that figure, knowing it was selling the property under market value. I have always tried to get the very best price for my clients. I strongly urged him to go to auction and I asked his permission to use the heading "Reserve Price Set at $95,000!" which he allowed me to do. I literally had dozens of buyers' clambouring for the property during the campaign, with most of them wanting to buy immediately. I advised my client to wait until Auction and not to consider selling beforehand, which he did.

On the night of the auction there were dozens of people wanting this property. Immediately prior to the auction the owner came up to me and said:

"Oh Maria! I had a beautiful dream last night! I dreamt that my house sold for $115,000!"

Well it did sell, but not for $115,000. It sold for $137,500! My owner was ecstatic! Now THAT'S what I get paid for. Not just selling the house, but really working out what is the most favourable strategy to get the very best result for my client.

Only last week I was paid the biggest compliment of my career. I received an email from a lady living in USA. The email read:

"Hi Maria,

I've been trying to find you. You sold my property at .... back in 2009. I need to sell my mother's house and I told my brothers if there is one person that will get us the best price it's Maria!"

This lady had searched through Google to find me. Wow! And I most certainly did remember her and I vividly remembered the auction I promoted and called for her. She was living in the USA back then also and family members were living rent free in her house. And they had trashed it. This was when I was working out of one of my own offices under a different banner, before I had decided to semi-retire (!). I assessed the value to be approximately $300,000 to $320,000 at that time taking into consideration the amount of work needed to bring this property back to a well presented state and I suggested auction to her, which she agreed to do. I marketed the property with the heading along the lines of "Renovate or Detonate!" and had an opening bid on the property of $270,000.

Immediately prior to the auction I received an offer on the property of $340,000 – an excellent price. By now this lady had returned to Australia for the actual auction. I can remember sitting on her mother's back porch showing her the signed contract at $340,000 and the 10% deposit cheque that I had brought with me. She asked me for advice, but I refused to give it to her – I told her that I didn't want to be responsible for the decision, it was her call. Cleverly, she reworded the question:

"Ok, so what would you do if you were me?" she asked

"Personally, I would wait for the auction." Was my reply. "But I'm not advising you to do that. And if you do decide to go to auction, we should still keep your reserve price at $320,000 as we've already discussed. So you may not get $340,000 on the day of the auction. And if I tell you not to take this offer and wait for the auction and your home only sells for $320,000, I could have just cost you $20,000!" I explained.

"I hear you. But you know what? I like what you said about waiting for the auction. If I lose money, well that's my fault, not yours." She kindly replied.

So the following Saturday we held the auction. And we sold her home for $375,000! And all these years later she wants me to work for her so much that she was willing to search for me!

Tips from this chapter:

1. **Choose a campaign that is really going to promote your property to all the buyers looking in your price range**

2. **Make sure the advertising really captures either the essence of your property or your determination to sell**

3. **If you are prepared to spend money getting your home looking "right" to the buyers, then also make sure that you don't skimp on its promotion**

4. **Work out a strategy with your agent – and if you don't like your ads get him to change them until your satisfied**

5. **Remember, a well-strategized campaign can bring you tens of thousands of dollars return**

Chapter 5:
Getting Ready for Auction

Organise a Contract for Sale

So you've made the decision and you've signed up for auction. What next? First and foremost you need to have a contract for sale before your property can be advertised, so you need to contact your solicitor to do this for you. Depending on the speed of your local Council, this document can be prepared in as little as two days or up to two weeks. Without this document you cannot promote your property, so get this ordered straight away.

Whilst this document is being prepared the agent will also get the marketing ready. If you have elected to get professional photography, Virtual Tours, floor plans and personalised signboards organised, then this is the time this should happen.

Get your home looking good!

My best advice to you, when getting your home ready for market, is to suggest this: if you were about to sell your car you would probably get it detailed before you advertise it. Think the same way about your property. Most homes today are beautifully presented, but I still come across those that aren't, and this can cost you thousands of dollars. There is nothing more off-putting to a buyer than the thought of cleaning up somebody else's mess. Sorry, but if I don't tell you, who will?

Over the years I have seen some really filthy houses! And yet these owners expect to get the same result as pristine clean homes. I have been through houses that have had dirty underwear strewn over bedroom floors (on the day of the auction too, I might add) and have had to kick stuff I'd rather not touch under beds!! I often shake my head with disbelief when this happens. I understand that we are all very busy people, and I understand that children and pets leave their debris behind them, but put yourself in the minds of the buyers. If you don't have the time to do this yourself, get a cleaner in! Most agents that have rent rolls will also have cleaners on their books that will give your home a good clean for just a few hundred dollars –

money well spent, I can assure you. Get windows and carpets cleaned, de-clutter your home, get the gardens trimmed, lawns cut, edges done, and weeding done. And please get this done BEFORE the photography is due so that the property is looking good before it ever comes on the market. If you leave it and only get it done for the day of the auction you have already missed the boat! Ask your agent if there is anything he would advise you to attend to, he'll tell you!

Dogs and cats in the house? Not a good idea when you are selling your home. Keep them and their "stuff" (i.e. beds and bowls) outside for at least the duration of the open house or reinspection. I love dogs, but they are smelly creatures even when they are bathed regularly. There are many people out there totally averse to keeping pets in the house and they can get very turned off your property.

Open for Inspection

It's Saturday, open house day. No doubt you have been thoroughly scrubbing up all week just for this half hour window of opportunity. I have heard owners advised to "brew coffee" "bake a cake" or "light scented candles" – I don't subscribe to these points of view. There are people that are allergic to certain scents or that are nauseated by the smell of coffee or baking. My suggestion is that your home should smell CLEAN! Cleaning agents, floor cleaners, disinfectants are far preferable aromas than anything else. If you are smokers or there have been pets in your home you really need to let the fresh air in and either get rid of or get cleaned any of the fabrics that can harbour these smells. Curtains are often culprits in holding in stale smells – get them washed or dry cleaned well in advance. Perfumes and baking smells will only mask a bad aroma, not get rid of it.

A tip for actors before they go onto stage is "check your nose and flies"! With a home I always suggest "check your toilets" before your open house, particularly if you have little ones!

In my opinion it is entirely up to you whether or not you want to be present whilst the open house is taking place. Many owners don't want to be there and will disappear for the duration, but if they ask me if I want them to leave then I tell them it's up to them. All I do advise is that they don't follow the buyers around trying to be helpful and that they don't engage buyers in long conversations about how great their property is. This often smacks of desperation, and this is not what we want the buyers to believe. If you decide not to be there rest assured we agents will look after your property like it is ours. We don't allow people to just open cupboard doors, drawers or closets. If they want a closer look at the size of any storage areas we suggest that they do a reinspection to do this.

I rarely hold an open home singlehandedly. Usually there at least two of us, one at the front door to take down buyers' details and one inside to answer questions and observe the behaviour of the buyers. Nevertheless, do not leave jewellery, money or small objects of value lying around, it can be too tempting. I have never had anything stolen at an open house in all these years, most people are extremely honest, but I never chance fate.

Personally I will not allow a buyer to enter an occupied home unless they have given me their name and contact details. Very occasionally I do come across people that strongly object to doing this (goodness knows why!) and they simply are not allowed to enter the premises. I also make sure I get buyers to take their shoes off on wet days or to walk on carpeted areas. Leaving old towels at the front and back doors on rainy days would be really useful for your agent. I also will not allow too many people through the property at the same time. There has to be a limit to how many people are in the property simply because a large crowd will make any property seem small and can be off-putting. How can you really see the home if you can't see beyond other peoples' bodies?!!

Generally speaking we try to get buyers' opinions when they walk back out of the house and this feedback is extremely important for you. If there have been droves of people through the home then we may have to wait until later that day or Monday to get that feedback. My standard practice is to both telephone the owner later that day/Monday to give them the numbers of inspections and to let them know how many people are interested in attending the auction. I will also send a written report to the owners during the course of the following week with the buyer's name, his opinion of value and his general comments about the property. This information can be invaluable. Remember, these buyers will be seeing everything in your price range and will be comparing properties. We agents see our stock, not the stock being promoted by our competition, so our vision is limited.

Assessing the Interest in your Home

As an agent I generally look at the number of contracts that have been issued for the property as a guideline to the volume of people that may be interested in coming to the auction. Usually when we are asking buyers what they think of the property we also ask them if they will be coming to the auction to bid. Generally we can pick the keen buyers and the half-hearted buyers at this stage, and this feedback we convey to you.

Sometimes we will get offers prior to the auction and I shall discuss this in greater depth in the next chapter. Obviously if people are making offers then they are keen and one would assume that they would be coming to the auction if their offer is declined.

Another good way to assess interest is from the pest and or building reports that are requested prior to the auction, although far more rare than it really should be. I have had many, many successful auctions where no reports are done whatsoever. I actually do advise buyers to get at least a pest report done, but they often don't listen to this advice! Of the 21 properties I sold under the hammer last year *less than half* had pest reports done on them before the auction! And very, very,

very occasionally a buyer might get a valuation done on the property.

Regardless of all this, you can get buyers turning up on the day of the auction that have never seen the property before that successfully bid and blow everyone else out of the water. This happens more frequently than not, and no longer surprises me as much as it used to. Like I said earlier, I have even experienced buyers buying off slides/videos that have never seen the property until they become the owners! Only with an auction ....

Tips from this chapter
1. **Get a Contract for Sale organised from your solicitor/conveyancer**
2. **Take advantage of this time lag to "put your house in order"**
3. **Get all the cleaning and repair work done before the photography is taken.**
4. **Ask your agent if there is anything he would advise you to attend to in particular**
5. **Bring in professional cleaners if you don't have time to freshen the house yourself**
6. **Keep pets outdoors during open house inspections and keep their "stuff" outside**
7. **Check the toilets before the open house starts**
8. **If you're staying home, don't follow the buyers around**
9. **Expect detailed feedback from the buyers – particularly written reports**
10. **Check the volume of contracts issued and reports done to assess the interest in your property**

Chapter 6: Considering Offers Prior to Auction

The most frequently asked question buyers ask is "how much will the owners take?" and this is why I never want the reserve price set until the week of the auction, because what the owner will take as opposed to what a competitive crowd may yield can be several thousands of dollars apart. If I tell a buyer what the owner wants it will either put him off completely or it could strongly influence his opinion of the property's value.

The whole point of an auction is to see how much buyers, with competition, will pay. I usually give buyers a general guideline with some examples of what has recently sold locally or I will give a guideline by saying "we're expecting a sale over …." I will then follow that up with "what is your price range?" If they are well under the owner's thinking, I will not encourage these buyers to come to the auction – why waste their time by getting their hopes too high?

Keen buyers will then try to buy prior to the auction and some will submit solid offers during the campaign. Their general thinking is to secure the property for themselves and to shut the door on their competition. However, the majority of buyers make offers that equate to a reality based price, not a dream price for the owner, which is what an auction is really all about.

For example, I recently had an auction where the owner told me at the point of listing that they would be more than happy with $620,000. We could have easily listed this property at say, $629,000 and had it sold within one day at $620,000. Instead of doing this I strongly urged them to take the property to auction. During the campaign I could see there were several really interested parties that really wanted to buy and it would have been easy to sell to any of them for $620,000 prior to the auction. The owner would have got what they wanted and I would have made a very quick sale. However, rather than do this I encouraged the owner to wait until the auction. We still set the reserve price at $620,000, and I brought the hammer down at $655,000 – a nice windfall for any owner. Had the owner not listened to my advice he would have sold for $620,000 and never known that he had missed out on $35,000!

When buyers ask me if an owner will sell before auction I always explain that for an owner to do this, he must be seduced by that offer, it must be in or very close to his Dream Price range. Then we go round in circles for a little bit whilst the buyer tries to pull the owner's price out of me and I try to pull his best price out of him. It's an inevitable dance which usually ends with the buyer making an offer. I generally then say "that's quite a reasonable offer but it may not seduce the owner to cancel everything and sell to you. However, he may willingly take this on the day" because I don't want to lose this buyer completely. We need as many bidders to attend the auction as possible. There will only be one buyer, the rest of the field will drive up the price.

I work for the owner, not the buyer, and my mission is to get the very best price out of the marketplace. The buyer's mission is to drive the price down or to eliminate the competition. However, I must submit all offers to the owners – that's the law – it is not for me to make decisions on behalf of the owners. I will always tell the owners what offers have been submitted not only because I am legally obliged to do so, but also this information is imperative when we sit and set the reserve price.

So when these offers are being made to you don't be disappointed. Many offers prior to an auction - even low offers – are an indication of how many people are interested in your property. The more the better. Most buyers still won't listen to the agent and will still make low offers – their mission is to push the price down. Not many buyers will submit their very best offer prior to an auction. In some instances, even **they** don't know what their very best price is until they are pushed by the competition.

I recently called an auction where a buyer came to the property on the first open house and was extremely keen to buy it and he indicated that he would pay $530,000, but wouldn't make an offer over this. The listing agent believed that the property was worth $530,000 to $550,000. The owner was happy to sell at $530,000 as he was committed to buying a business and this price allowed him to fulfil his obligations. Following the agent's advice the owner didn't accept the offer of $530,000 prior to the auction but he did set the reserve price at $530,000. On the day of the auction there were only four registered bidders, the keen buyer, two half-hearted buyers and a completely new contender that had not viewed the property before that day. The bidding started slowly and it was like pulling teeth until I announced that the property was on the market when we eventually hit $530,000. Suddenly the new contender started to bid and would not let go! His final and winning bid was $611,000, and the very keen bidder's last bid was $610,000! He had gone $80,000 OVER what he offered prior to auction! However, I do believe that had he made an offer of $580,000 prior to the auction, the owner would have been tempted to take this. I doubt when he was making his offer he never even dreamt that under pressure he would have gone to $610,000.

When a good offer comes along before an auction, it is the hardest thing as an agent to advise an owner one way or another. This must be entirely your choice. However, I really do believe that if there has been a lot of interest in the property and several contracts have been handed out there is a strong possibility that the auction will yield more. I am always far more inclined to suggest that an owner waits for the auction rather than sells beforehand, but it's not my money that I am risking. As in the example in Chapter 4, had that owner accepted the offer of $340,000, which was $20,000 over what she was hoping to get, she would have missed out on a sale price of $375,000! Her decision earned her and extra $35,000 – big money.

As you can see, I am a devotee of waiting til the day rather than making a quick sale. I can really only remember, over all these years and over all these sales, when an owner sold to the same buyer that offered prior to the auction for a lesser figure, and that lesser figure was only down by $1,000.

So when you are presented with a good offer make sure you find out from your agent how many buyers there are on your property. Check with your agent, or from the reports he has sent you, how many inspections have been done on your property. Ask him how many contracts have been issued. If this offer is at or very close to your Dream Price, then do give it serious consideration. Ask yourself if you will find it easy to live with the consequences should you reject this offer and then sell for less.

If you do decide to accept this offer, don't take your property off the market or cancel any of the open houses until your buyer has presented you with an unconditionally signed contract and the 10% deposit. DO NOT accept a contract with a cooling-off period. This would only be useful to the buyer, not you. And, just to be on the safe side, instruct your agent NOT to tell any of the other buyers that you have taken an offer. If this buyer gets remorse and changes his mind, you don't want to have lost other buyers' interest.

Please remember that an agent can be heavily fined or lose his licence if he encourages gazumping. This means he cannot go to all the other interested parties and tell them the amount that you've just been offered to try and get more. If you are thinking like this, then reject this offer and wait for the auction.

Here is another cautionary tale: many buyers will do almost anything to find out what the owner will take. I had a listing several years ago that I was auctioning. We were at the end of the campaign and we had a reasonable amount of interest in the property even though we were in a flat market at the time. The owner rang me the week of the auction and he was really upset. I asked him what was wrong and he said:
"One of the buyers came back last night and knocked on the door. He wanted to have another look through. I'd seen him at the open house so I thought it'd be OK without getting you out here." He said.

"That's your choice, but I would have been happy to come if you rang me. But what's upset you so much?" I replied.

"Well, I showed him around for a bit and then he said "I'm thinking of paying $180,000 for this, is that OK?" *and I said* "No it bloody well isn't! I won't sell for a cent under $220,000!" *If that's all he's thinking why are you letting him come to the auction?"* He exploded, angrily.

My owner had fallen for the oldest trick in the book. Throw an offer at the owner and if he is naïve or if you catch him off guard, he will tell you what he wants to get for the property! I smoothed down my owner and told him this, nicely. The outcome? This buyer came to the auction and paid $225,000 for the property.

The moral of the story is simple. Keep your reserve price or your expectations to yourself. Tell no-one and do not be lured into giving the game away. If someone throws an offer at you do not over-react! Should buyers come to your property without an appointment it is your choice whether or not you are willing to let them in, but if you're paying an agent a selling fee then it is more than reasonable to expect the buyer to inspect with the agent. If a buyer does turn up out of hours, sure let him inspect if you want to, but don't get drawn into talking about the price. Some buyers will try to "win you over" hoping that if you like them you will sell it them before the auction or for a cheaper amount. Don't be swayed by this! This is your chance to maximise your return: you don't owe anyone any favours. And be careful who you confide in – neighbours and friends might know interested parties!!!

Tips from this chapter:

1. All buyers will want to know how much you want and if you'll sell before auction. It is their mission to push your price down, it is your agent's mission to get you the best price.

2. Don't be disappointed by low offers before the auction. The competition between the buyers will bring the best price regardless of what they say before the auction.

3. If you are too tempted and you do take an offer prior to auction, it MUST be an unconditional offer with a 10% deposit. DO NOT TAKE YOUR PROPERTY OFF THE MARKET WHILST THIS SALE GOES THROUGH.

4. Don't expect your agent to ring all other interested parties to try and drive the price up. Firstly, it is illegal for an agent to encourage gazumping. Secondly if this buyer gets remorse and doesn't proceed it could ruin your chance at auction.

5. Be careful that you are not lured to give away what your anticipated reserve price will be. Don't overreact to silly offers.

6. Don't be charmed into a sale. This is your opportunity to maximise your return and you are not obliged to do anyone any favours.

Chapter 7:
Setting your Reserve Price

Reserve Price

All agents work in different ways, but I prefer to leave setting the reserve price to the week of the auction. I think it is imperative to really study the feedback from the buyers and to intelligently work out a strategy.

At the point of listing there would have been a discussion about the price range the agent believed your property fell into and you would have given him your expectations. His opinion would have been recorded on the front page of your agency agreement. I think it is most important to refer back to this. Unless there have been some severe economic changes in the marketplace since this was done, such as interest rate rises, these figures should still be relevant. If the interest rates have just dropped that may not automatically raise your price. There is always a knee-jerk reaction to rates going up but not down, and it is a viable reaction. If the interest rates rise, then a buyer's buying power goes down. Fear also plays a part in the buyer's mind – "will I afford my loan if the rates keep rising?" etc.

I will never forget driving down to the Masonic Hall in Liverpool in June 1989 for our auction night. I had three listings myself that night and there were collectively a further twelve properties going to the auction block. We had several buyers on all of our properties and we were gearing up for a fantastic night. The auctions were starting at 7 pm. I was driving down to the venue to prepare the room and the 6 o'clock news came on the car radio. Interest rates had just risen to 17%! BANG! In one instant the market collapsed and we then went into "the recession we had to have". NOT ONE of our properties sold that night. NOT ONE! The buyers that did turn up didn't make a bid. Every single property was passed in with no bids. I had never seen anything like it. It totally scared me.

It took a long time to recover from this marketplace. There were many repossessed properties coming onto the market and the prices were falling away badly. Auctions were still a good way to sell, PROVIDED THAT the reserve prices were set sensibly.

And even in a hot market, which we are enjoying right now in Australia, the reserve prices must still be set sensibly. Just because you have seen droves of people going through your property don't be fooled into making your Dream Price your reserve price.

It is better to discuss your reserve price with your agent in the privacy of your home or their office before the day of the auction where there are no prying ears and you can be very open with your conversation. I always speak with every person that has inspected this property prior to this meeting. I will be very direct and ask them if they intend to attend the auction and if they intend to bid. They will then give me a very direct response; yes they are coming and they will be bidding; they are coming to observe but will not be bidding or they are not coming at all. I usually have a list of names in front of me and I colour code the responses. This gives me a quick reference to the definite number of buyers that are coming and that intend to bid. More often than not the keener buyers have had their solicitors contact the owners' solicitors to alter some of the conditions in the contract or to alter the deposit amount. They may also have had pest and building inspections done on the property, but not always. In fact more often than not, no reports will be done.

The best advice I can give you at this stage is stick to the game plan. Don't move the goal posts unless you have really changed your mind about selling. The ideal reserve price should act as a trigger for competitive bidding so it needs to be set at the lower end of the Reality range. In fact what you should do is seriously consider the very, very lowest price you are prepared to accept and **SET THAT** as your reserve price.

Why? Like I said, you want this to act as a trigger. Many people attend auctions, register to bid and do nothing until the Auctioneer declares "this is on the market, I'm selling today". Once this declaration is made a surprising number of people then start bidding. There is no guarantee, however. If the bidding stops at that figure, you are **SOLD** and you have to accept this is what the buying public believe your property is worth today. **You cannot refuse to sell once your reserve price is hit**.

The volume of inspections can be a good yardstick to see how popular your style of home is with current buyers, but volume doesn't always mean vast numbers of people registering to bid. One recent auction listing I had in Turramurra brought in 45 inspections, over 20 contracts were issued on the property (thank goodness for email otherwise we would have annihilated a small forest!) yet on the day of the auction there were only seven registered bidders. The vendor was sensible, we stuck to the game plan and kept the reserve price low, and we ended up with $95,000 over that reserve price, which was a further $45,000 more than what we both agreed we would like the property to sell for. The winning buyer was involved in the bidding from the get-go, but two bidders didn't join in until the property was on the market, which then drew the best price out of that buyer.

If you are reluctant to take a risk or if you prefer to make your final decision whilst the property is being auctioned, then set a higher reserve price than the figure you are being advised to set it at by your agent, but be prepared to drop down from that during the auction if the bidding stops and you are happy to take the last bid offered. Getting your property on the market is absolutely crucial to not only making a sale, but in getting the juice out of your buyers. So many times the bidding stops prior to that reserve price, the owners then put the property on the market and it fires up the bidding once more. There is no guarantee that this will happen, but here are a few examples:

1. Vendor advised that reserve price should be set at $700,000. Reserve price set at $735,000. Bidding stopped at $700,000. Vendor put property on the market **new bidder stepped in at this stage** and property sold for $706,000.

2. Vendor advised that reserve price should be set at $500,000. Reserve price set at $550,000. Bidding stopped at $521,000. Vendor put property on the market and property sold for $530,000.

3. Vendor advised that reserve price should be set at $510,000. Reserve price set at $540,000. Bidding stopped at $515,000. Vendor put property on the market, **new bidder stepped in at this stage** and property sold for $536,000.

As you can see from the above example, new bidders stepped in **once the property was on the market.** Had these owners not dropped their reserve prices and allowed the property to be passed in, chances are they would not have gotten the final price because the competition would have then reverted to being between buyer and seller, not between buyer and buyer.

I believe that the setting of the reserve price is actually indicative of how much an owner trusts his agent. If you believe in your agent, then also believe that he is determined to get you your very best price. Why? Well commercially he will use your result to impress other owners thinking of selling (not surprisingly many would-be sellers attend auctions to see how an agent will perform) and when the public see success they will give their business to that agent. They won't be impressed if they feel that the property undersold. More importantly, good agents have a professional pride in what they do. For them it's not just about making a sale, but it's also the self-satisfaction that no-one else could have done a better job. "Tradesmen" agents probably wouldn't even have suggested auction to you; "Carpenter" agents just want the hammer to come down; "Cabinet Maker" agents take a real pride to go above and beyond their clients expectations, with the way the marketing is done, the way the campaign is organised, in getting the very, very best price for their clients and then, finally to take away all obstacles between the exchange of contracts to moving out day. So what type of agent have you chosen?

As an auctioneer my greatest thrill is to go way above reserve price for the owners. When I called auctions for other agents I would always have a discussion with each owner prior to the auction starting, whether the auctions were in rooms or on site. I wanted to make sure that their agent had covered everything with them and I also wanted to reassure them that I never bring the hammer down quickly. Never. I need to know myself that there is not another cent out there that I haven't captured. The highest amount I have ever achieved over reserve price is $600,000!! The final sale figure was actually almost double the reserve price and my proudest moment as an auctioneer! What is important to note here is that this particular property had had two independent Valuers submit valuations on this property and the owners based their reserve price on these expert opinions.

I will discuss later about dropping your reserve price as the auction is underway, but the time to discuss this between partners in the property is from the time you have set the reserve price to the actual auction taking place. Really nut out the absolute minimum you are prepared to take – don't leave this undiscussed until the auction is happening! Good old scouting adage: "Be Prepared". Better this discussion is superfluous and the bidding sails past your reserve rather than having to make tough, hard decisions in the moment.

Dropping your Reserve Price at Auction

I always run through all scenarios with my owners before the day of the auction, and the most important ground I believe I need to cover, even if I get a reserve price that I am happy with, is what can happen on the day if we don't reach that reserve price.

The bidding stops: we are say just a few thousand dollars short of that reserve; I stop the auction and seek my owner's instructions. Decision time. Can I call this property "On the market" and make the sale, or do I pass it in? This really is a most critical decision. Some owners believe that they are better off passing the property in and negotiating with the highest bidder after the auction: **ABSOLUTELY NOT!** In all the times I have had this happen I find that the buyers are less likely to improve their offer significantly after the auction. They feel that they are back in the driving seat and become more entrenched in their price. But worse than this, you are only negotiating with one buyer – the rest of the field are shut out.

A really good example of this I recorded in my first book "Auction Success – Top 10 Tips to Successfully Buy a Property @ Auction". One of my vendors went to an auction to buy once I had unconditionally exchanged her sale. She stopped bidding for a particular property at $585,000 – the reserve price wasn't reached. Like all good agents, the selling agent then went between buyer and seller and told my client that if she increased her bid by $1,000 to $586,000 the owner would put the property on the market. She did as directed, the Auctioneer declared her increased bid and declared the property was "on the market." Then a person in the crowd who wasn't even registered at that point, indicated that he wanted to bid. The Auctioneer, correctly, stopped the auction, allowed the new contender to register and then accepted his bid of $590,000! My vendor couldn't afford to go higher than this bid and consequently missed out on the property.

Getting the property "on the market" during the auction is so much more effective to draw out the best price rather than trying to negotiate after the auction. In the above example had that bidder not gone the extra $1,000 before the end of the auction and the owner had been rigid in not dropping the reserve price to $585,000, the new contender would never have gotten involved and the owner would have missed out on a further $4,000.

Vendor Bid

As I have mentioned before, I really don't like using this unless I absolutely have to. I consider that the only time I need to draw on this is if the bidding has stopped too far away from the reserve price and negotiating with the under bidder and the owner hasn't reached a positive conclusion.

The only other time I want to use a Vendor Bid is if there is only one registered bidder. I have sold a considerable number of auctions under the hammer where this has happened. Usually what will happen is they make an opening bid, I counter with a vendor bid, and they bid again at a figure the owner will accept. If the bidder doesn't make an opening bid, then I will make the opening bid with the Vendor Bid and then declare that the next bid will be the buying bid.

Consequently I always advise my vendors that I want to be able to call a Vendor Bid and then declare that the next bid will be the buying bid, otherwise it is extremely difficult to get another bid.

Another thing to note is that if a property is passed in and any one enquires "what did the property get passed in at?" in New South Wales we cannot declare the Vendor Bid, but we have to declare the actual bid made by the last buyer.

Tips from this chapter:

1. Remember: your Reserve Price should act like a trigger to the bidding, not the brakes!

2. Don't move the goalposts unless you don't want to sell!

3. When setting your reserve price go back to the agency agreement and refer to the prices discussed at the start of the campaign.

4. Don't get carried away because you have seen volumes of buyers go through your property – so many owners get over excited and make their Dream Price their reserve price.

5. Have some faith in your agent and your auctioneer – just remember top professionals want a great result too!

6. Always have a Plan B so that you have a fall-back position if the reserve price isn't reached and get this well and truly discussed BEFORE the auction.

7. Don't think in terms of getting a good result by negotiating after the auction – do everything in your power to get the property on the market before the property get passed in.

8. Be prepared to drop your Reserve Price if you have to.

9. Always discuss a Vendor Bid with your agent or with the auctioneer – make sure the auctioneer can declare the property on the market on the very next bid.

Chapter 8:

Auction Day

So this is it, the day of the Auction has finally arrived – how exciting! If you are holding your auction on site there will usually be an open house immediately prior to the auction. If you are part of a group of auctions that are being held in rooms, this will normally occur on a week night – often a Thursday night, at a particular venue.

With on-site auctions when the property is marketed there will be a time as well as a date that the auction will commence. With in-rooms auctions there will be a venue and a general time advertised, but the Order of Sale for the properties may not be available before that evening.

On site Auctions are usually started promptly at the time advertised, although there could be a delay for whatever reason.

A buyer may be stuck in traffic and phone ahead and request that the Auctioneer delay proceedings and wait for them, or even the Auctioneer may be running late if they too get caught in traffic and are running between auctions. Whatever the reasons, there could be a delay, but usually that would only be for a few minutes.

In rooms Auctions, however, will usually start very promptly. If there are several properties on the Auction block on the same night, the Auctioneer must be very conscious of the time to get through all the stock. I have called over twenty auctions in one night, and, as the proceedings started at 7 pm and the hall closed at 11.30 pm promptly, I had to make sure I got through all the stock very efficiently.

When creating an Order for Sale for in-room auctions, most agencies will select their most popular properties to begin the evening and to end the evening. The preferable order is to have the first three properties to sell to set the mood for the evening, then in the middle have the least popular and then to keep the absolutely most popular property for the last auction. We want to keep the crowd in the room!

So if you see that your property is either first or last on the list for the night, it should mean that your agent is extremely confident you are going to sell. If your property is situated in the middle then maybe there is a slight lack of confidence.

With in-room auctions there is usually a video played of each house prior to the auctioneer making reference to the contract and commencing the auction. I have attended many in-room auctions where buyers that have missed out on a previous property start bidding on a property just from these videos! In fact I have sold literally dozens of properties in-rooms sight unseen. It's amusing that when buyers get in the mood to buy, they will do this!

I have also had many on-site auctions where a buyer has turned up on the day of the auction, never seen the house before, and has registered, bid and won the property. Obviously to do this they must be financially well prepared and have a great deal of confidence in the market place.

Registering to Bid

First of all if anyone wishes to bid at an Auction in NSW, they need to register and to do this they need to have i.d. that will show their current place of residence and a photo of themselves. If they are electing to have someone else bid for them, both names, their i.d. and the i.d. of the person bidding for them need to be registered. They also have to give the Auctioneer an Authority that this person is bidding on their behalf. The ideal i.d. is a current Drivers Licence. If the buyer doesn't have one, then a utility bill with their name and current address plus some form of photo i.d. is acceptable – maybe a club membership card, or passport. Here in NSW if you do not hold a Drivers Licence you may obtain a voluntary Photocard to prove your identity. These are available from the Roads & Maritime Services at the local RTA office.

If the buyers are purchasing with partners such as a spouse, parent, sibling etc. then only one of them needs to register, not all parties. However all parties do need to sign the contract if they are the successful bidders.

Just remember, buyers do not have to bid just because they have registered, but a buyer certainly cannot bid if they are not registered! Auctioneers can be fined thousands of dollars if they accept a bid from an unregistered bidder! They don't make this mistake, I can assure you!

Once registered, the buyer will be given a number. This number is exclusive to them and must be shown every time they make their bid. Every Auctioneer in NSW today has an assistant recording each bid – it is a legal requirement. The bids are recorded by writing down the number of the bidder and the amount he has bid.

Before the start of your auction your agent or your auctioneer will come over to you and let you know how many buyers have registered to bid on your property. The more the better, but don't be disappointed if it's less than you were expecting – you may still get a terrific result.

Auction Warning Signs

Before the start of the Auction, whether on site or in rooms, the Auction Warning Signs must be on display. In some States, they need to be on display for a specific amount of time, depending on the State's bye laws governing auction.

Some Auctioneers read out these rules, some don't. Personally, I do and the reason I do this is because I know I work in an area where English is the second language to most people, and even though they may be fluent in speaking English this does not necessarily mean they can read English.

I will now go through rules that apply in NSW individually with an explanation for each point:

1. **The Auctioneer must have the Reserve Price in writing prior to the commencement of the Auction.**

This is self-explanatory. If I don't have this, I don't call an Auction. I have had owners tell me on several occasions to "just call the Auction – I'll let you know if I'm selling". No, sorry, no can do. I am not risking my licence on an instruction that is contrary to the law

The reserve price that the owner sets can move down during an Auction, but never up. From an Auctioneer's point of view I prefer a realistic Reserve Price which is gauged from buyer feedback during the Auction campaign. However, many owners like to inflate the reserve price so that they can make their final decision on what they will take as the Auction is actually being called. This may mean that I have to stop the Auction and consult with the Vendor if the bidding stops before the Reserve Price is reached.

2. **The Vendor is allowed one Vendor Bid only. If this bid is used the Auctioneer must announce in a clear and precise manner that this bid is on behalf of a Vendor.**
Personally I don't like using a Vendor Bid because this is usually the death knell of an Auction, but on occasions I will use it, provided that I can also state that the next bid will be the buying bid. That is up to the Vendor. I will discuss the use of a Vendor Bid prior to the Auction and I will usually set this with each Vendor as a fall-back position if I need to use it.

3. **The highest bidder is deemed to be the purchaser, subject to the reserve price.**

Again, self- explanatory. If the property is "On the market" this means that the reserve price has been reached and if the bidding stops at any point thereafter the property is sold.

4. **In the event of a disputed bid, the auctioneer is the sole arbitrator and the auctioneer's decision shall be final.**

If one person claims a bid was theirs and that is contrary to the bids recorded I have the authority to declare who the bid was taken from. No-one can argue with this. I can also refuse to accept a bid which I deem is not in the best interest of the Vendor. What does this mean? Well, if a bidder appears to be intoxicated I will not take his bid.

Also, I can set the pace of the Auction by refusing small bids that are far away from market value or the reserve price. For example: if a property has a reserve price of $600,000 and a bidder opens at $400,000, I will then call for a bid of say $420,000 or $450,000 immediately after. If someone bids $401,000, I can refuse that. I will set the increments that I wish to raise the bidding.

5. **A bidder is taken to be a principal unless before bidding the bidder has given to the auctioneer a copy of a written authority to bid for or on behalf of another person.**

Should the buyer bring someone to the Auction to bid on their behalf all parties have to be registered, the bidder has to be nominated and the auctioneer has to be given an authority in writing from the buyer that they want this person to bid for them.

If the buyer cannot attend the Auction on Auction day they can still bid by telephone. To do this they need to register (which can be done any time prior to the Auction date) and they can nominate a real estate agent or friend to bid on their behalf with themselves on the other end of the phone giving instructions. Again, the nominated bidder will also have to register, but it will still be the buyer signing the contract. Arrangements will have to be made with the owner's permission, as to when the contract can be signed.

6. **A bid cannot be accepted after the fall of the hammer.**

An Auctioneer can be fined several thousands of dollars if they accept a bid once the hammer comes down. I often have bidders trying to play cat and mouse with me – why, I'll never know! But they leave it right up until I am at the third and final call before they make their move. Although I do draw out waiting for a buyer, I cannot let that be for too long. I never bring the hammer down quickly, but I cannot give preferential treatment to a bidder that is agonisingly slow in making a decision.

7. **As soon as practicable, after the fall of the hammer, the purchaser is to sign the agreement for sale.**

The successful bidder is escorted to a table to then sign the contract and pay the agreed deposit. Regardless of how much information we agents give buyers, there will always be a rogue one that gets to this point and tells us that they are buying on behalf of their child/brother/uncle and that these people have to sign the contract, not the bidder. Not acceptable. Whoever registered to bid has to sign the contract. They can put "or Nominee" on the contract and if that leaves them liable to pay extra Stamp Duties, that's their bad luck. Otherwise this contract is invalid and should the buyers change their mind, there is no penalty and you are left with a house unsold.

Should this occur and the buyer refuses to sign the contract but wants you to wait until the relative turns up, refuse to do so. Refuse to sell them the property and instruct your agent to go to the under bidder and take his offer. Otherwise you are extremely vulnerable right up until the point of settlement.

At every Auction I call I also announce the deposit rule, which is:

Unless before bidding the bidder has been granted a request by the vendor to place less than 10% deposit on the day, the vendor can refuse to sell the bidder the property.

Although I have already dealt with this, I will go over it again: The successful bidder's options to pay the deposit are either by personal cheque, bank cheque or Deposit Guarantee Bond. I have had bidders turn up to Auctions with plastic bags full of cash, I have to say, but in this day and age I would refuse to accept large sums of cash – it leaves us way too vulnerable to theft. Most agencies are only insured for a limited amount of cash stolen (approximately $2,000 per day) so if we take possession of tens of thousands of dollars, we are liable and responsible for that money until it is banked! One agent I know had a deposit of $80,000 stolen from the person doing the banking in the middle of the High Street in the middle of the day! And he had to cover this loss himself!!

The other disadvantage of taking wads of cash are that we then have to sit and count it – not a time friendly activity if we are calling another Auction straight after this one!

What I do want to emphasise however, is that if several requests are made of you prior to the start of the auction to exchange on a lesser figure than 10%, I would advise you to do so, otherwise you are eliminating bidders. The more bidders eligible to bid, the better the result should be and that is in your favour, not the buyer's.

The Actual Auction

So the time has come for the actual auction to commence. What should you expect? First of all I suggest you position yourself in a place that is discreetly out of the way so that you can witness all the proceedings and yet still be very accessible if your agent or auctioneer needs to seek your instructions. I also suggest that where you are positioned is separate from the bidders so that any conversations you may have remain confidential.

Obviously all auctioneers have their own methodology, but generally speaking they will call the crowd to order and welcome them to your property. With In rooms auctions they will play the videos of your home. They may read out the terms of purchasing at auction and they will then refer to your Contract for Sale and read out general information such as settlement time (standard is 42 days from exchange to settlement), inclusions in the sale (i.e. dishwasher, clothes line, TV antenna etc.)

Once these formalities are over, the auctioneer will then call for an opening bid. I am going to deal with the actual bidding process later, but there are a couple of things I wish to tidy up now. There are basically two differing styles of auctioning. They are the English Auction, or open ascending price auction (which is the most popular style these days) and the Dutch Auction or open descending price auction. The difference between these two styles is that with the English Auction the bidding starts low and is worked upwards by the Auctioneer and with the Dutch Auction the Auctioneer calls out high figures and then drops these down until someone starts to bid. I much prefer the English Auction and work from low to high. I don't like the other method at all. When I call an auction I am not concerned at how low the bidding starts, I am looking for participation more than anything else, and then setting the tempo of the bidding.

Tips from this chapter:

1. On site auctions will commence straight after the last open house; In rooms auctions will take place at a nominated venue, usually on a week night.

2. With an on site auction position yourself so that the agent and/or auctioneer can access you to gain your instructions if necessary. Choose a location that is convenient for this but also positions you to observe all the activities.

3. With In rooms auctions the order of sale can be a good indication on how much confidence your agent has that your property will sell under the hammer. If your home is one of the first or the very last then your agent is very confident. In the middle possibly means he is not so confident.

4. Buyers can emerge from the crowd and can bid, buy and surprise everyone – this will only happen with an auction listing.

5. All buyers must be registered before they can bid, and they must hold up their unique number so that their bids can be recorded.

6. The Auction Warning Signs must be on display prior to the start of the auction. Some auctioneers will read them out, but not always.

7. These Bye Laws must be adhered to or they can jeopardise the sale. Agents and auctioneers can be heavily fined if they do not follow the rules.

8. Be very reasonable with the amount of deposit or settlement times (if possible) to allow as many bidders to participate in the auction as possible.

9. Don't allow the successful bidder to then try to arrange for an absent party to buy your property if they haven't observed the rules and done all the necessary registering that they needed to do – this could mean that your exchange is invalid and the buyers can pull out right up until the day of settlement without losing their deposit!

10. If your Auctioneer is using the English Auction method – that is starting low and rising with each bid, do not be alarmed if the bidding starts off low. Your auctioneer just needs participation at the beginning of the auction and to then set the tempo of the auction. This is vital.

Chapter 9:
The Bidding

This is probably the most important aspect of an auction and the most difficult to determine. Every single auction I have called (and that's probably hitting the thousands now) is completely unique. However, I shall try to capture as much information as I can for you so that you will see all scenarios and nothing will surprise you on the day.

First of all I want to say this: The absolutely worst thing that can happen to you is that the house doesn't sell under the hammer. **THIS IS NOT THE END OF THE WORLD!** I have seen owners get so psyched up over an auction that they are almost sick with worry until the whole thing is over. Regardless of your need to sell, **CHILL!** Provided that you have listened to your agent's advice, haven't moved the goal-posts, and have set a sensible reserve price, there is every chance your property will sell. If it doesn't sell at the actual auction, then take heart in the fact that most properties that don't sell under the hammer will probably sell within three weeks of the auction.

No Registered Bidders

First of all, if there are no registered bidders, there is no auction. Many owners (and agents) are devastated by this, but it can happen. If this happens to you there really needs to be a meeting with you and the agent to work out why this happened. Have there been changes in the marketplace? Did your auction date conflict with a long weekend or a sporting event? Was too high an opening bid put on your property? Is your property unusual or in a difficult location that put buyers off? Set a date to have this meeting but not immediately after the auction. Give your agent time to contact the parties that had expressed interest that were a no show and get their feedback as to why they didn't attend. Then put a sensible price on the property and start advertising it as a Private Treaty sale. You will get a result.

Registered Bidders but No Bids

Regardless of the methodology of the auctioneer (i.e. whether he uses the English Auction or the Dutch Auction), there needs to be a starting bid from a registered bidder to kick the whole thing off. Occasionally an agent will have advertised an "opening bid..." or "bidding starting from..." and that figure will be called out by the auctioneer. Most auctions do not have opening bids and the auctioneer has to wait for a figure to be called from the bidders. The majority of auctions start with deathly silence as the Auctioneer is calling for that first bid and waits for the crowd's response. And they wait. And they wait. And they wait.

Now occasionally we have auctions that do have attendees that register, yet still no-one bids and the property has to be passed in. Passing a property in with no bids is preferable to passing it in with a very low bid recorded. The reason I say this is because when we market the property after the auction, enquiring buyers will often ask "What was the property passed in at?" A low figure could influence their thinking and perception of its value.

Registered Bidders that Bid

So eventually the auctioneer has coaxed a bid out of the bidders and the auction slowly starts. I can honestly say that at the beginning of an auction, I really don't care how low the buyers start the bidding – all I am looking for at this stage is their participation so I can get the whole thing to roll along. Just remember that the bidders are probably even more nervous than you at this time. Not many of us want to draw attention to ourselves and bidding at an auction can be very intimidating.

Auctioneers will steer an auction by suggesting the increments they want from the bidders. So if the bidding starts really low, I may be calling for the next bid to be $50,000 or $20,000 more. Once I get close to reserve I shall then look at taking lower increments, maybe $10,000 or $5,000 bids. When I get within $20,000 of reserve, I could then be calling for bids of $2,000 or $1,000 – sometimes even $500 bids, depending on the strength of the bidders. My job is to get to reserve price, whatever that may be. I will not make a judgement call on market value of the property – that is not my responsibility. Once I reach that reserve figure, I will then allow virtually anything, but I have never been an Auctioneer that will allow increments of under $500. We are selling property, not cattle!

Once the tempo is established the bidding can be relatively swift, but not always. There may be several contenders at the beginning, but eventually this could fade to just two or three bidders. Seasoned bidders, if they really want the property, will throw in strong bids - $10,000, $20,000 etc. to put their opponents off. And other seasoned bidders may respond back with just $1,000 bid to show they are not put off. Each bid will be acknowledged by the auctioneer and recorded by their assistant. Even if you cannot see what is going on, you will definitely hear it. And you will also be aware when the bidding slows down and stops.

If the Reserve Price is reached
Once the reserve price is reached, declaring the property "On the Market!" is at the discretion of the auctioneer. What I normally do, if we have sailed past the reserve price, is wait until the bidding has slowed down before I make this declaration. I don't want people to be put off bidding – I want the competition to gather momentum. But when it does slow down I will say *"It's on the Market! I am selling today! Make no mistake, if there is no further bidding I'm bringing the hammer down on this one and it will be SOLD!"* Often this fires up the bidding

again, but the bids are usually small at this stage, although I have seen buyers throw in big bids to knock out the competition, and that often works. What can also happen is that new contenders start to bid once they know they can now buy the property. I have had many auctions where the actual buying bids are made by buyers that haven't made a bid until the property is well and truly on the market and I am just about to bring the hammer down.

After the bidding has completely finished and under-bidders are shaking their heads that they no longer wish to continue bidding, I will "Call" three times and then finally say "Are you all silent? Are you all done? Then this property is SOLD!" I have to be very careful at this stage, and I do take my time, because once the gavel (hammer) hits the table, board, or newspaper that I may be holding, I cannot take another bid. If an auctioneer does he can be heavily fined! So if there are any late bidders they could miss out – more importantly, you could miss out on more money! An auctioneer's job is to sell the property for as much money as he can get for the owner – so I don't bring the hammer down quickly. I want to get the juice out of the buyers for all my owners!

After the hammer comes down and the brouhaha has calmed down, the buyers are then invited to sign the contract and pay the agreed deposit.

What happens if the Reserve Price isn't reached?
Ok, so in the above scenario, your property is sold, however, if the bidding stops before the Auctioneer declares that the property is "On the market …" it means that the bidding hasn't reached the reserve price. What will normally happen then is that the agent and or Auctioneer will consult you to see what you want to do. If you are willing to drop your reserve price to this last bid figure to sell, and instruct the Auctioneer to do this, the Auctioneer will declare that the property is "On the Market!" Sometimes this may then kick the bidding on and other contenders may start bidding again. Otherwise the Auctioneer has permission to sell at this last bid price.

The agent or the Auctioneer will do their utmost to bring the last bidder and you together before the fall of the hammer. So there could be a lot of work by the agent or the Auctioneer, going back and forth between the last bidder and yourself, and this is why I suggested that you should be accessible, but out of earshot of the bidders. At this point you have to make a crucial decision. If you refuse to accept the last bid or offer, your property will be passed in and all negotiations will be done with the last person to bid only. This then eliminates the rest of the field. I can rattle off heaps of examples where owners have bitten the bullet, put the property on the market, and then sold at a great price, so be very careful if you have to make this decision.

If an agreement is made between both parties, the Auctioneer will state that "the buyer has increased his offer to ...... and the property is now on the market, I am selling today!" This doesn't mean that the property has sold, because anyone else can now throw in a bid, and often they do.

But if you are not willing to sell at the price the bidding has stopped at and the buyer will not increase his offer to a figure acceptable to you, the Auctioneer will state that if there are no further bids he will "Pass In" the property. When this happens, then the last bidder has the first right to negotiate with you after the Auction and that buyer will still buy under Auction conditions, which means he signs the contract, pays the agreed deposit and the property is sold unconditionally.

If no agreement can be made with this bidder, the agent will then approach any of the other under-bidders to see if they are willing to pay a figure that you will take. Don't think for one minute that negotiating after the auction is stronger than negotiating before the auction finishes. All the pressure is on the buyer before the property is passed in to him. Afterwards, he is more likely to feel that he is in the driving position. And don't forget, passing in a property eliminates the rest of the field. I know it seems strange that buyers will continue to bid or start to participate in bidding only if the property is on the market, but in actuality, this happens all the time.

If the bidding has stopped way under your reserve price, for whatever reason, or if there is only one person bidding on your property, then the auctioneer may use the Vendor Bid. This should be discussed well prior to the auction, usually when you are setting the reserve price. Like I advised before, the best way for the Vendor Bid to act as a trigger is to allow the auctioneer to announce that the next bid will be the buying bid, so set this Vendor Bid accordingly.

Your property can sell under auction conditions with a registered bidder up until 12 midnight of the day of the auction. If an unregistered bidder wants to buy during this period and none of the registered bidders are interested, then you can sell the property, but under cooling-off conditions only.

If there is no chance of an immediate sale, then you will have to put an asking price on the property and proceed to market as a Private Treaty listing. Should this occur, don't despair! You will probably be sold within the next two or three weeks! The only thing that will stop this is if you have been and still are, far too rigid on the price you are expecting to sell for.

Tips from this chapter:

1. It is not the end of the World if your property doesn't sell at auction! On average you will be sold within the next two to three weeks.

2. If there are no registered bidders there is no auction and it will be cancelled. Then arrange a meeting with your agent so that you can analyse why this occurred and how you proceed from here. Same applies if there are registered bidders, but no-one bids.

3. Be prepared to drop your reserve price should the bidding stop before this is reached. A sale under the hammer is unconditional and the buyer is committed to the sale with a large deposit which he would have to forfeit to you should he change his mind after the auction. Also, auction conditions are "Buyer Beware!" there can be no further negotiations after an auction. Your property is SOLD!

4. Should the property not reach the reserve price and be passed in, the under bidder has the first right to negotiate before any other bidders are approached. This is not a strong way for a seller to negotiate – the buyer is back in the driving seat. Bite the bullet on your price, get your property on the market – the bidding could kick off again!

5. If the final bid is way under reserve price, the auctioneer can use your Vendor Bid. Make sure you have set this before the auction starts so that there is no delay. Also make sure that your auctioneer can announce that the next bid will be the buying bid once this is announced.

6. Your property can sell under auction conditions up until midnight the day of your auction. After that it is sold

with a cooling off contract and is not an unconditional sale. If the buyer is not registered for your auction, he can only buy under cooling off conditions.

7. Should no sale eventuate from the auction, then set a price that your property can be marketed at, and do this quickly. Often buyers will be ringing the agent immediately after the auction for information on your property.

8. DO NOT DESPAIR! Many, many, many sales occur within three weeks of the auction date if the property doesn't sell under the hammer.

Chapter 10: What Happens Next?

So the hammer came down and you are successfully sold! Congratulations! Job well done! Now what happens?

The buyers will be ushered to a table to sign the contract whilst the rest of the field vacate the property – the show is over. With In rooms auctions there is usually a side office where this is performed. The first job is to seal the deal by getting the contracts exchanged, and the quicker this is done the better.

The agent will write down the buyers' details on the front page of the contract together with their solicitor's details. They will also write in the sale price at the appropriate space on the front page of the contract and they will get the buyer to sign this document. If more than one party are buying the property then they all have to sign this document. If a Company is buying then a Company Director will have to sign this document. The deposit is then paid by whichever method and whatever amount has been agreed upon and the buyer will be issued with a receipt for that.

Once the buyer(s) have signed and paid that deposit, you, the owners will sign a second contract, if one is available. If for some reason there is only one document, all parties can sign this, although it is not desirable. But anything can happen at an auction. Sometimes a prospective buyer will ask to look at the contract prior to the auction and then inadvertently walk off with it in his pocket. I have to say this has never happened to me, but it can happen and if it does it throws a spanner in the works!

Once all parties have signed the documents and the deposit is paid both contracts are dated with that day's date. That is it. You have just sold your property! The agent will usually take both contracts with him, do his necessary paperwork and then send your signed contract to the buyers' solicitor and their signed contract to your solicitor. You will probably receive a letter in the post the next week from the agent both congratulating you on the transaction and to confirm the amount of money they are holding.

You can now start to pack!

Prior to settlement the buyers are entitled to conduct a final inspection. At that point they can walk through the property and look for any damage or any missing inclusions that may have happened or been taken after the exchange of the contract. They cannot argue about issues or damages that were like that at the time of the auction - that was up to them to notice - but anything afterwards should be addressed by you, the vendor.

The agent will accompany them on this inspection and will act as witness to the proceedings. Also, they should be able to expect any rubbish to be removed from the site by the owner. Most owners are very obliging and leave their home in immaculate condition, but occasionally we do get some minor issues that need to be addressed, and this can be done through your solicitor at this time. Once this is done settlement will take place.

In most cases the agents are the stakeholders for the 10% deposit and this money is safely deposited into a Trust Account. This money can only be released prior to settlement for the purchase of another property and can only be paid into another Trust Account. Trust Account monies are not eligible for interest. Should both parties want this money invested until settlement, which can happen where there is a delay in settlement, then both the buyers and the sellers need to supply the agent with their Tax File Numbers.

The standard time frame from exchange until settlement is usually 42 days. The acting solicitors will arrange between themselves the actual settlement date and they will inform you once this is established.

All the keys to access the property and remotes for garage doors, security gates etc. need to be with the agent prior to settlement unless other arrangements have been made between all parties. No keys should be handed out by the agent to the buyer before settlement takes place. Sometimes there can be a delay in the settlement for a variety of reasons and if settlement is postponed then the buyer should be denied access to the property unless this is specifically allowed by the owner. Agents cannot just assume a settlement has taken place just because it was scheduled for a specific day and time, they must check and make sure it has happened.

Once settlement has happened the agent needs to obtain Orders from both parties' solicitors. These Orders will then allow him to subtract his commission from the deposit he is holding in his Trust Account and then supply you with the balance of these funds. This can either be sent out to you by cheque or they can be electronically transferred into your account. Don't forget to give your agent these instructions and to supply him with the necessary details to make this happen.

Once more, Congratulations on the Sale of your Property! I hope you found this information useful.

Tips from this chapter:

1. Once the hammer comes down it is imperative that the contracts are signed and exchanged and the agreed deposit is paid according to either the contract or specific agreement.

2. The signed contracts will be sent out to respective solicitors the very next working day by the agent and written confirmation will be sent to you. You can now start to pack!

3. The buyer will probably be advised to do a final inspection very close to the settlement date. This actual date will be organised by the respective solicitors.

4. The buyer is entitled to reimbursement for any damage done to the property after the auction, and is entitled to take possession of the property in a clean state with all rubbish removed. The agent will accompany the buyer for this inspection and act as a witness.

5. Once the agent receives the Orders from both solicitors he will then deduct his commission and forward you the balance by either cheque or electronic transfer. Don't forget to give the agent your instructions and details for this to occur.

GLOSSARY OF TERMS

1. **Agent.** The person acting on behalf of the vendor

2. **Agreement for Sale.** Or Contract for Sale. The legal document usually prepared by a legal advisor (solicitor or conveyancer) which must be available before a property can be marketed

3. **Auction.** A public sale in which goods or property are sold to the highest bidder

4. **Auctioneer.** A person who conducts auctions by accepting bids and declaring goods sold

5. **Bidder.** Any person registered to bid at an Auction

6. **Buyer Beware.** The Golden Rule of Auction which puts the responsibility on the buyer that if he purchases at Auction, he buys "as is"

7. **Caveat Emptor.** The Latin version of above

8. **Deceased Estate.** The owner of the property has died and the property is being sold by either the beneficiaries or the Public Trustee

9. **Dutch Auction** or open descending price auction – the auctioneer calls or high bids and then drops and drops until a bid is made

10. **English Auction** Or open ascending price auction – currently the most popular form of auction.

    The auctioneer begins from a low opening bid and brings the bidding up in increments determined by him/her to the reserve price and possibly beyond.

11. **Fall of the Hammer**   Or hammer comes down. When the Auctioneer hits the gavel on the table, or anything else, which indicates that the property is sold

12. **On the Market**   The reserve price has been reached and the Auctioneer has the authority to sell the property to the highest bidder

13. **Open House**   An allotted time, usually on a Saturday, when the property is open to the Public to inspect without an appointment

14. **Opening Bid**   An indication of where bidding will start for a property. This is usually 10-20% under the anticipated reserve price or the owner's ideal sale price

15. **Mortgagee in Possession**   When the lending body has taken possession from an owner for non-payment of their mortgage

16. **Passed In**   The reserve price hasn't been reached and the owner refuses to sell at the last bid price

17. **Reserve Price**   Usually the least amount the Vendor is willing to take at Auction to allow a sale to ensue. This must be given to the Auctioneer in writing before the start of the Auction

18. **Registration**   It is law in NSW today that all bidders must be registered and to do this they must show photographic id with their current address to the selling agent, who will then record these details and issue that person with a unique number which must be shown as a bid is made.
Auctioneers can be heavily fined if they take a bid from an unregistered bidder, however this bid is still deemed to be valid

19. **Vendor Bid**   A bid made by the Auctioneer on behalf of the Vendor

About the Author

Maria Lawrance

Maria Lawrance started her career in Real Estate in September 1986. She is a Licensed Real Estate Agent and an Accredited Auctioneer, and has won many awards in her career.

Back in 1989 Maria was the first woman in her then Franchise Group to win Salesperson of the Year and she had to beat 86 men to do it! It is an accolade she held for almost twenty years before another lady took that title. She also won Auction Lister of the Year in the same year, first person to ever do both !

Back in 1987 Maria participated in an Auction Listing training course and was one of the first people to introduce the Auction system to her area. Now she has literally thousands of auctions under her belt, both as an Auction lister and as a highly respected Auctioneer. She has

Auctioned property all over Sydney and has conducted both on site auctions and in-room auctions.

Maria sold the last of the three offices she owned in April 2011 with the intention of retiring. Len Pretti, a well known guru in Property Management, coaxed her to join his businesses. It didn't take much! Maria loves her work.

Even as a veteran of the real estate industry, Maria has some of the best results around. She has just sold her 100th property since joining Len's team two short years ago. Her conversion rate of listings to sales stands at 93%. But she is most proud of her statistic for Agent's opinion to sale price which currently stands at 99.83%! And her average time on market for those 100 sales is 5.2 weeks!

This year alone Maria has achieved some amazing results for property owners, with her best result being $600,000 over reserve price for one particular property!

She now wants to share her knowledge and her experience with the marketplace to leave a legacy in the industry she has proudly served for over 27 years.

There has never been a book written before to help sellers navigate through the Auction system. And with the useful tips and hints you will find in these pages, you should now be able to sell with confidence

Follow Maria: **www.marialawrance.com.au**

"like" us on
facebook

AUCTION
SUCCESS

TOP 10 TIPS TO
SUCCESSFULLY
BUY PROPERTY
@ **AUCTION**

LEADING AUSTRALIAN AUCTIONEER & AGENT

MARIA LAWRANCE

First Edition 2014 | Copyright 2014 by Maria Lawrance

ISBN-10:   0992416523
ISBN-13: 978-0-9924165-2-2